This Crocheting log book

BELONGS TO:

_ _ _ _ _ _ _ _ _

DEDICATION

This Crocheting Log book is dedicated to all the Crocheter's out there who love to make and share all their needlework creations, and document their findings in the process.

You are my inspiration for producing books and I'm honored to be a part of keeping all of your yarn and needle notes organized in one easy to find spot.

How to use this Ultimate Crochet Journal:

This ultimate Crochet Project notebook is a perfect way to track and record all your crocheting activities.

This unique review log book is a great way to keep all of your important information all in one place.

Each interior page includes prompts and space to record the following:

1. Project Number - Write which number project you are working on.

2. Project Name - Record the project name.

3. Created For - Write what person you are making this for.

4. Start Date - Keep track of your projects by entering the date it was started.

5. End Date - Record the date completed.

6. Hook - Stay on task by entering the crochet hook size.

7. Pattern - Use this box to label which pattern is being made, hat, headband, blanket...etc.

8. Design Source - Record your inspiration, simple shapes, stitches used.

9. Gauge - Write out the number of stitches per inch and rows per inch...so as to be reminded later..

10. Extra Tools - Keep track of measuring tape, rulers, stitch markers, scissors and so forth...

11. Yarn Type - Stay on task by labeling the yarn color, brand, dye lot, and Skeins.

12. Yarn Sample/Label - Attach a yarn sample, or label here.

13. Sketch/Photo - Blank Space to draw out a sketch or attach a photo of the current project.

If you are new to crocheting or have been at it for a while, this Crochet Project Journal is a must have! Can make an awesome gift for craft and crochet hobby lovers! Convenient size of 8x10 inches, 110 pages, quality white paper, soft matte finish cover, paperback.

Enjoy!

PROJECT #	HOOK
PROJECT NAME	PATTERN
CREATED FOR	DESIGN SOURCE
START DATE	GAUGE
END DATE	EXTRA TOOLS

YARN TYPE

✧ COLOR(S)	🏷 BRAND	||||| DYE LOT #	🧵 SKEINS

YARN SAMPLE/LABEL

ATTACH YARN SAMPLE / LABEL HERE

SKETCH / PHOTO

PROJECT #		HOOK	
PROJECT NAME		PATTERN	
CREATED FOR		DESIGN SOURCE	
START DATE		GAUGE	
END DATE		EXTRA TOOLS	

YARN TYPE

✦ COLOR(S)	🏷 BRAND	|||| DYE LOT #	SKEINS

YARN SAMPLE/LABEL

ATTACH YARN SAMPLE / LABEL HERE

SKETCH / PHOTO

PROJECT #		HOOK	
PROJECT NAME		PATTERN	
CREATED FOR		DESIGN SOURCE	
START DATE		GAUGE	
END DATE		EXTRA TOOLS	

YARN TYPE

COLOR(S)	BRAND	DYE LOT #	SKEINS

YARN SAMPLE/LABEL

ATTACH YARN SAMPLE / LABEL HERE

SKETCH / PHOTO

PROJECT

PROJECT NAME

CREATED FOR

START DATE

END DATE

HOOK

PATTERN

DESIGN SOURCE

GAUGE

EXTRA TOOLS

YARN TYPE

COLOR(S)	BRAND	DYE LOT #	SKEINS

YARN SAMPLE/LABEL

ATTACH YARN SAMPLE / LABEL HERE

SKETCH / PHOTO

	PROJECT #			HOOK
	PROJECT NAME			PATTERN
	CREATED FOR			DESIGN SOURCE
	START DATE			GAUGE
	END DATE			EXTRA TOOLS

YARN TYPE

COLOR(S)	BRAND	DYE LOT #	SKEINS

YARN SAMPLE/LABEL

ATTACH YARN SAMPLE / LABEL HERE

SKETCH / PHOTO

PROJECT #		HOOK
PROJECT NAME		PATTERN
CREATED FOR		DESIGN SOURCE
START DATE		GAUGE
END DATE		EXTRA TOOLS

YARN TYPE

COLOR(S)	BRAND	DYE LOT #	SKEINS

YARN SAMPLE/LABEL

ATTACH YARN SAMPLE / LABEL HERE

SKETCH / PHOTO

PROJECT #		HOOK
PROJECT NAME		PATTERN
CREATED FOR		DESIGN SOURCE
START DATE		GAUGE
END DATE		EXTRA TOOLS

YARN TYPE

COLOR(S)	BRAND	DYE LOT #	SKEINS

YARN SAMPLE/LABEL

ATTACH YARN SAMPLE / LABEL HERE

SKETCH / PHOTO

PROJECT #		HOOK	
PROJECT NAME		PATTERN	
CREATED FOR		DESIGN SOURCE	
START DATE		GAUGE	
END DATE		EXTRA TOOLS	

YARN TYPE

COLOR(S)	BRAND	DYE LOT #	SKEINS

YARN SAMPLE/LABEL

ATTACH YARN SAMPLE / LABEL HERE

SKETCH / PHOTO

PROJECT #		HOOK
PROJECT NAME		PATTERN
CREATED FOR		DESIGN SOURCE
START DATE		GAUGE
END DATE		EXTRA TOOLS

YARN TYPE

COLOR(S)	BRAND	DYE LOT #	SKEINS

YARN SAMPLE/LABEL

ATTACH YARN SAMPLE / LABEL HERE

SKETCH / PHOTO

	PROJECT #			HOOK
	PROJECT NAME			PATTERN
	CREATED FOR			DESIGN SOURCE
	START DATE			GAUGE
	END DATE			EXTRA TOOLS

YARN TYPE

✦ COLOR(S)	🏷 BRAND	||||| DYE LOT #	SKEINS

YARN SAMPLE/LABEL

ATTACH YARN SAMPLE / LABEL HERE

SKETCH / PHOTO

PROJECT #		HOOK	
PROJECT NAME		PATTERN	
CREATED FOR		DESIGN SOURCE	
START DATE		GAUGE	
END DATE		EXTRA TOOLS	

YARN TYPE

✧ COLOR(S)	🏷 BRAND	||||| DYE LOT #	🧶 SKEINS

YARN SAMPLE/LABEL

ATTACH YARN SAMPLE / LABEL HERE

SKETCH / PHOTO

PROJECT #		HOOK	
PROJECT NAME		PATTERN	
CREATED FOR		DESIGN SOURCE	
START DATE		GAUGE	
END DATE		EXTRA TOOLS	

YARN TYPE

COLOR(S)	BRAND	DYE LOT #	SKEINS

YARN SAMPLE/LABEL

ATTACH YARN SAMPLE / LABEL HERE

SKETCH / PHOTO

	PROJECT #			HOOK
	PROJECT NAME			PATTERN
	CREATED FOR			DESIGN SOURCE
	START DATE			GAUGE
	END DATE			EXTRA TOOLS

YARN TYPE

COLOR(S)	BRAND	DYE LOT #	SKEINS

YARN SAMPLE/LABEL

ATTACH YARN SAMPLE / LABEL HERE

SKETCH / PHOTO

	PROJECT #		HOOK
	PROJECT NAME		PATTERN
	CREATED FOR		DESIGN SOURCE
	START DATE		GAUGE
	END DATE		EXTRA TOOLS

YARN TYPE

COLOR(S)	BRAND	DYE LOT #	SKEINS

YARN SAMPLE/LABEL

ATTACH YARN SAMPLE / LABEL HERE

SKETCH / PHOTO

PROJECT #		HOOK	
PROJECT NAME		PATTERN	
CREATED FOR		DESIGN SOURCE	
START DATE		GAUGE	
END DATE		EXTRA TOOLS	

YARN TYPE

COLOR(S)	BRAND	DYE LOT #	SKEINS

YARN SAMPLE/LABEL

ATTACH YARN SAMPLE / LABEL HERE

SKETCH / PHOTO

PROJECT #		HOOK
PROJECT NAME		PATTERN
CREATED FOR		DESIGN SOURCE
START DATE		GAUGE
END DATE		EXTRA TOOLS

YARN TYPE

✦ COLOR(S)	🏷 BRAND	▥ DYE LOT #	🧶 SKEINS

YARN SAMPLE/LABEL

ATTACH YARN SAMPLE / LABEL HERE

SKETCH / PHOTO

PROJECT #		HOOK	
PROJECT NAME		PATTERN	
CREATED FOR		DESIGN SOURCE	
START DATE		GAUGE	
END DATE		EXTRA TOOLS	

YARN TYPE

COLOR(S)	BRAND	DYE LOT #	SKEINS

YARN SAMPLE/LABEL

ATTACH YARN SAMPLE / LABEL HERE

SKETCH / PHOTO

PROJECT #		HOOK
PROJECT NAME		PATTERN
CREATED FOR		DESIGN SOURCE
START DATE		GAUGE
END DATE		EXTRA TOOLS

YARN TYPE

COLOR(S)	BRAND	DYE LOT #	SKEINS

YARN SAMPLE/LABEL

ATTACH YARN SAMPLE / LABEL HERE

SKETCH / PHOTO

	PROJECT #			HOOK
	PROJECT NAME			PATTERN
	CREATED FOR			DESIGN SOURCE
	START DATE			GAUGE
	END DATE			EXTRA TOOLS

YARN TYPE

COLOR(S)	BRAND	DYE LOT #	SKEINS

YARN SAMPLE/LABEL

ATTACH YARN SAMPLE / LABEL HERE

SKETCH / PHOTO

PROJECT #		HOOK	
PROJECT NAME		PATTERN	
CREATED FOR		DESIGN SOURCE	
START DATE		GAUGE	
END DATE		EXTRA TOOLS	

YARN TYPE

COLOR(S)	BRAND	DYE LOT #	SKEINS

YARN SAMPLE/LABEL

ATTACH YARN SAMPLE / LABEL HERE

SKETCH / PHOTO

	PROJECT #			HOOK
	PROJECT NAME			PATTERN
	CREATED FOR			DESIGN SOURCE
	START DATE			GAUGE
	END DATE			EXTRA TOOLS

YARN TYPE

COLOR(S)	BRAND	DYE LOT #	SKEINS

YARN SAMPLE/LABEL

ATTACH YARN SAMPLE / LABEL HERE

SKETCH / PHOTO

PROJECT #		HOOK	
PROJECT NAME		PATTERN	
CREATED FOR		DESIGN SOURCE	
START DATE		GAUGE	
END DATE		EXTRA TOOLS	

YARN TYPE

COLOR(S)	BRAND	DYE LOT #	SKEINS

YARN SAMPLE/LABEL

ATTACH YARN SAMPLE / LABEL HERE

SKETCH / PHOTO

PROJECT #		HOOK	
PROJECT NAME		PATTERN	
CREATED FOR		DESIGN SOURCE	
START DATE		GAUGE	
END DATE		EXTRA TOOLS	

YARN TYPE

✧ COLOR(S)	🏷 BRAND	‖‖‖ DYE LOT #	🧶 SKEINS

YARN SAMPLE/LABEL

ATTACH YARN SAMPLE / LABEL HERE

SKETCH / PHOTO

PROJECT #		HOOK	
PROJECT NAME		PATTERN	
CREATED FOR		DESIGN SOURCE	
START DATE		GAUGE	
END DATE		EXTRA TOOLS	

YARN TYPE

COLOR(S)	BRAND	DYE LOT #	SKEINS

YARN SAMPLE/LABEL

ATTACH YARN SAMPLE / LABEL HERE

SKETCH / PHOTO

	PROJECT #			HOOK
	PROJECT NAME			PATTERN
	CREATED FOR			DESIGN SOURCE
	START DATE			GAUGE
	END DATE			EXTRA TOOLS

YARN TYPE

✦ COLOR(S)	BRAND	DYE LOT #	SKEINS

YARN SAMPLE/LABEL

ATTACH YARN SAMPLE / LABEL HERE

SKETCH / PHOTO

PROJECT #		HOOK	
PROJECT NAME		PATTERN	
CREATED FOR		DESIGN SOURCE	
START DATE		GAUGE	
END DATE		EXTRA TOOLS	

YARN TYPE

COLOR(S)	BRAND	DYE LOT #	SKEINS

YARN SAMPLE/LABEL

ATTACH YARN SAMPLE / LABEL HERE

SKETCH / PHOTO

	PROJECT #		HOOK
	PROJECT NAME		PATTERN
	CREATED FOR		DESIGN SOURCE
	START DATE		GAUGE
	END DATE		EXTRA TOOLS

YARN TYPE

COLOR(S)	BRAND	DYE LOT #	SKEINS

YARN SAMPLE/LABEL

ATTACH YARN SAMPLE / LABEL HERE

SKETCH / PHOTO

PROJECT #		HOOK	
PROJECT NAME		PATTERN	
CREATED FOR		DESIGN SOURCE	
START DATE		GAUGE	
END DATE		EXTRA TOOLS	

YARN TYPE

✦ COLOR(S)	🏷 BRAND	||||| DYE LOT #	🧶 SKEINS

YARN SAMPLE/LABEL

ATTACH YARN SAMPLE / LABEL HERE

SKETCH / PHOTO

PROJECT #	**HOOK**
PROJECT NAME	**PATTERN**
CREATED FOR	**DESIGN SOURCE**
START DATE	**GAUGE**
END DATE	**EXTRA TOOLS**

YARN TYPE

COLOR(S)	BRAND	DYE LOT #	SKEINS

YARN SAMPLE/LABEL

ATTACH YARN SAMPLE / LABEL HERE

SKETCH / PHOTO

PROJECT #		HOOK
PROJECT NAME		PATTERN
CREATED FOR		DESIGN SOURCE
START DATE		GAUGE
END DATE		EXTRA TOOLS

YARN TYPE

COLOR(S)	BRAND	DYE LOT #	SKEINS

YARN SAMPLE/LABEL

ATTACH YARN SAMPLE / LABEL HERE

SKETCH / PHOTO

PROJECT #		HOOK	
PROJECT NAME		PATTERN	
CREATED FOR		DESIGN SOURCE	
START DATE		GAUGE	
END DATE		EXTRA TOOLS	

YARN TYPE

COLOR(S)	BRAND	DYE LOT #	SKEINS

YARN SAMPLE/LABEL

ATTACH YARN SAMPLE / LABEL HERE

SKETCH / PHOTO

PROJECT #		HOOK	
PROJECT NAME		PATTERN	
CREATED FOR		DESIGN SOURCE	
START DATE		GAUGE	
END DATE		EXTRA TOOLS	

YARN TYPE

✧ COLOR(S)	🏷 BRAND	▥ DYE LOT #	🧶 SKEINS

YARN SAMPLE/LABEL

ATTACH YARN SAMPLE / LABEL HERE

SKETCH / PHOTO

PROJECT #		HOOK
PROJECT NAME		PATTERN
CREATED FOR		DESIGN SOURCE
START DATE		GAUGE
END DATE		EXTRA TOOLS

YARN TYPE

COLOR(S)	BRAND	DYE LOT #	SKEINS

YARN SAMPLE/LABEL

ATTACH YARN SAMPLE / LABEL HERE

SKETCH / PHOTO

PROJECT #		HOOK	
PROJECT NAME		PATTERN	
CREATED FOR		DESIGN SOURCE	
START DATE		GAUGE	
END DATE		EXTRA TOOLS	

YARN TYPE

COLOR(S)	BRAND	DYE LOT #	SKEINS

YARN SAMPLE/LABEL

ATTACH YARN SAMPLE / LABEL HERE

SKETCH / PHOTO

PROJECT #		HOOK
PROJECT NAME		PATTERN
CREATED FOR		DESIGN SOURCE
START DATE		GAUGE
END DATE		EXTRA TOOLS

YARN TYPE

COLOR(S)	BRAND	DYE LOT #	SKEINS

YARN SAMPLE/LABEL

ATTACH YARN SAMPLE / LABEL HERE

SKETCH / PHOTO

PROJECT #		HOOK
PROJECT NAME		PATTERN
CREATED FOR		DESIGN SOURCE
START DATE		GAUGE
END DATE		EXTRA TOOLS

YARN TYPE

COLOR(S)	BRAND	DYE LOT #	SKEINS

YARN SAMPLE/LABEL

ATTACH YARN SAMPLE / LABEL HERE

SKETCH / PHOTO

PROJECT #		HOOK	
PROJECT NAME		PATTERN	
CREATED FOR		DESIGN SOURCE	
START DATE		GAUGE	
END DATE		EXTRA TOOLS	

YARN TYPE

COLOR(S)	BRAND	DYE LOT #	SKEINS

YARN SAMPLE/LABEL

ATTACH YARN SAMPLE / LABEL HERE

SKETCH / PHOTO

PROJECT #		HOOK
PROJECT NAME		PATTERN
CREATED FOR		DESIGN SOURCE
START DATE		GAUGE
END DATE		EXTRA TOOLS

YARN TYPE

COLOR(S)	BRAND	DYE LOT #	SKEINS

YARN SAMPLE/LABEL

ATTACH YARN SAMPLE / LABEL HERE

SKETCH / PHOTO

PROJECT #		HOOK	
PROJECT NAME		PATTERN	
CREATED FOR		DESIGN SOURCE	
START DATE		GAUGE	
END DATE		EXTRA TOOLS	

YARN TYPE

COLOR(S)	BRAND	DYE LOT #	SKEINS

YARN SAMPLE/LABEL

ATTACH YARN SAMPLE / LABEL HERE

SKETCH / PHOTO

PROJECT #		HOOK	
PROJECT NAME		PATTERN	
CREATED FOR		DESIGN SOURCE	
START DATE		GAUGE	
END DATE		EXTRA TOOLS	

YARN TYPE

✦ COLOR(S)	🏷 BRAND	||||| DYE LOT #	🧶 SKEINS

YARN SAMPLE/LABEL

ATTACH YARN SAMPLE / LABEL HERE

SKETCH / PHOTO

PROJECT #		HOOK	
PROJECT NAME		PATTERN	
CREATED FOR		DESIGN SOURCE	
START DATE		GAUGE	
END DATE		EXTRA TOOLS	

YARN TYPE

COLOR(S)	BRAND	DYE LOT #	SKEINS

YARN SAMPLE/LABEL

ATTACH YARN SAMPLE / LABEL HERE

SKETCH / PHOTO

PROJECT

PROJECT NAME

CREATED FOR

START DATE

END DATE

HOOK

PATTERN

DESIGN SOURCE

GAUGE

EXTRA TOOLS

YARN TYPE

COLOR(S)	BRAND	DYE LOT #	SKEINS

YARN SAMPLE/LABEL

ATTACH YARN SAMPLE / LABEL HERE

SKETCH / PHOTO

PROJECT #		HOOK	
PROJECT NAME		PATTERN	
CREATED FOR		DESIGN SOURCE	
START DATE		GAUGE	
END DATE		EXTRA TOOLS	

YARN TYPE

COLOR(S)	BRAND	DYE LOT #	SKEINS

YARN SAMPLE/LABEL

ATTACH YARN SAMPLE / LABEL HERE

SKETCH / PHOTO

PROJECT #		HOOK	
PROJECT NAME		PATTERN	
CREATED FOR		DESIGN SOURCE	
START DATE		GAUGE	
END DATE		EXTRA TOOLS	

YARN TYPE

COLOR(S)	BRAND	DYE LOT #	SKEINS

YARN SAMPLE/LABEL

ATTACH YARN SAMPLE / LABEL HERE

SKETCH / PHOTO

	PROJECT #			HOOK
	PROJECT NAME			PATTERN
	CREATED FOR			DESIGN SOURCE
	START DATE			GAUGE
	END DATE			EXTRA TOOLS

YARN TYPE

COLOR(S)	BRAND	DYE LOT #	SKEINS

YARN SAMPLE/LABEL

ATTACH YARN SAMPLE / LABEL HERE

SKETCH / PHOTO

PROJECT #		HOOK
PROJECT NAME		PATTERN
CREATED FOR		DESIGN SOURCE
START DATE		GAUGE
END DATE		EXTRA TOOLS

YARN TYPE

COLOR(S)	BRAND	DYE LOT #	SKEINS

YARN SAMPLE/LABEL

ATTACH YARN SAMPLE / LABEL HERE

SKETCH / PHOTO

PROJECT

PROJECT NAME

CREATED FOR

START DATE

END DATE

HOOK

PATTERN

DESIGN SOURCE

GAUGE

EXTRA TOOLS

YARN TYPE

COLOR(S)	BRAND	DYE LOT #	SKEINS

YARN SAMPLE/LABEL

ATTACH YARN SAMPLE / LABEL HERE

SKETCH / PHOTO

	PROJECT #			HOOK
	PROJECT NAME			PATTERN
	CREATED FOR			DESIGN SOURCE
	START DATE			GAUGE
	END DATE			EXTRA TOOLS

YARN TYPE

✦ COLOR(S)	🏷 BRAND	▥ DYE LOT #	🧶 SKEINS

YARN SAMPLE/LABEL

ATTACH YARN SAMPLE / LABEL HERE

SKETCH / PHOTO

PROJECT #		**HOOK**	
PROJECT NAME		**PATTERN**	
CREATED FOR		**DESIGN SOURCE**	
START DATE		**GAUGE**	
END DATE		**EXTRA TOOLS**	

YARN TYPE

COLOR(S)	BRAND	DYE LOT #	SKEINS

YARN SAMPLE/LABEL

ATTACH YARN SAMPLE / LABEL HERE

SKETCH / PHOTO

PROJECT #		HOOK	
PROJECT NAME		PATTERN	
CREATED FOR		DESIGN SOURCE	
START DATE		GAUGE	
END DATE		EXTRA TOOLS	

YARN TYPE

COLOR(S)	BRAND	DYE LOT #	SKEINS

YARN SAMPLE/LABEL

ATTACH YARN SAMPLE / LABEL HERE

SKETCH / PHOTO

PROJECT #		HOOK	
PROJECT NAME		PATTERN	
CREATED FOR		DESIGN SOURCE	
START DATE		GAUGE	
END DATE		EXTRA TOOLS	

YARN TYPE

COLOR(S)	BRAND	DYE LOT #	SKEINS

YARN SAMPLE/LABEL

ATTACH YARN SAMPLE / LABEL HERE

SKETCH / PHOTO

PROJECT #		HOOK
PROJECT NAME		PATTERN
CREATED FOR		DESIGN SOURCE
START DATE		GAUGE
END DATE		EXTRA TOOLS

YARN TYPE

COLOR(S)	BRAND	DYE LOT #	SKEINS

YARN SAMPLE/LABEL

ATTACH YARN SAMPLE / LABEL HERE

SKETCH / PHOTO

PROJECT #		HOOK	
PROJECT NAME		PATTERN	
CREATED FOR		DESIGN SOURCE	
START DATE		GAUGE	
END DATE		EXTRA TOOLS	

YARN TYPE

COLOR(S)	BRAND	DYE LOT #	SKEINS

YARN SAMPLE/LABEL

ATTACH YARN SAMPLE / LABEL HERE

SKETCH / PHOTO

PROJECT #		HOOK	
PROJECT NAME		PATTERN	
CREATED FOR		DESIGN SOURCE	
START DATE		GAUGE	
END DATE		EXTRA TOOLS	

YARN TYPE

COLOR(S)	BRAND	DYE LOT #	SKEINS

YARN SAMPLE/LABEL

ATTACH YARN SAMPLE / LABEL HERE

SKETCH / PHOTO

	PROJECT #		HOOK
	PROJECT NAME		PATTERN
	CREATED FOR		DESIGN SOURCE
	START DATE		GAUGE
	END DATE		EXTRA TOOLS

YARN TYPE

COLOR(S)	BRAND	DYE LOT #	SKEINS

YARN SAMPLE/LABEL

ATTACH YARN SAMPLE / LABEL HERE

SKETCH / PHOTO

PROJECT #		HOOK	
PROJECT NAME		PATTERN	
CREATED FOR		DESIGN SOURCE	
START DATE		GAUGE	
END DATE		EXTRA TOOLS	

YARN TYPE

COLOR(S)	BRAND	DYE LOT #	SKEINS

YARN SAMPLE/LABEL

ATTACH YARN SAMPLE / LABEL HERE

SKETCH / PHOTO

PROJECT #		HOOK	
PROJECT NAME		PATTERN	
CREATED FOR		DESIGN SOURCE	
START DATE		GAUGE	
END DATE		EXTRA TOOLS	

YARN TYPE

COLOR(S)	BRAND	DYE LOT #	SKEINS

YARN SAMPLE/LABEL

ATTACH YARN SAMPLE / LABEL HERE

SKETCH / PHOTO

	PROJECT #			HOOK
	PROJECT NAME			PATTERN
	CREATED FOR			DESIGN SOURCE
	START DATE			GAUGE
	END DATE			EXTRA TOOLS

YARN TYPE

✧ COLOR(S)	🏷 BRAND	||||| DYE LOT #	SKEINS

YARN SAMPLE/LABEL

ATTACH YARN SAMPLE / LABEL HERE

SKETCH / PHOTO

PROJECT #		HOOK	
PROJECT NAME		PATTERN	
CREATED FOR		DESIGN SOURCE	
START DATE		GAUGE	
END DATE		EXTRA TOOLS	

YARN TYPE

COLOR(S)	BRAND	DYE LOT #	SKEINS

YARN SAMPLE/LABEL

ATTACH YARN SAMPLE / LABEL HERE

SKETCH / PHOTO

PROJECT #		HOOK	
PROJECT NAME		PATTERN	
CREATED FOR		DESIGN SOURCE	
START DATE		GAUGE	
END DATE		EXTRA TOOLS	

YARN TYPE

COLOR(S)	BRAND	DYE LOT #	SKEINS

YARN SAMPLE/LABEL

ATTACH YARN SAMPLE / LABEL HERE

SKETCH / PHOTO

PROJECT #		HOOK
PROJECT NAME		PATTERN
CREATED FOR		DESIGN SOURCE
START DATE		GAUGE
END DATE		EXTRA TOOLS

YARN TYPE

COLOR(S)	BRAND	DYE LOT #	SKEINS

YARN SAMPLE/LABEL

ATTACH YARN SAMPLE / LABEL HERE

SKETCH / PHOTO

PROJECT #		HOOK	
PROJECT NAME		PATTERN	
CREATED FOR		DESIGN SOURCE	
START DATE		GAUGE	
END DATE		EXTRA TOOLS	

YARN TYPE

COLOR(S)	BRAND	DYE LOT #	SKEINS

YARN SAMPLE/LABEL

ATTACH YARN SAMPLE / LABEL HERE

SKETCH / PHOTO

PROJECT #		HOOK	
PROJECT NAME		PATTERN	
CREATED FOR		DESIGN SOURCE	
START DATE		GAUGE	
END DATE		EXTRA TOOLS	

YARN TYPE

COLOR(S)	BRAND	DYE LOT #	SKEINS

YARN SAMPLE/LABEL

ATTACH YARN SAMPLE / LABEL HERE

SKETCH / PHOTO

PROJECT #		HOOK
PROJECT NAME		PATTERN
CREATED FOR		DESIGN SOURCE
START DATE		GAUGE
END DATE		EXTRA TOOLS

YARN TYPE

COLOR(S)	BRAND	DYE LOT #	SKEINS

YARN SAMPLE/LABEL

ATTACH YARN SAMPLE / LABEL HERE

SKETCH / PHOTO

PROJECT #		HOOK
PROJECT NAME		PATTERN
CREATED FOR		DESIGN SOURCE
START DATE		GAUGE
END DATE		EXTRA TOOLS

YARN TYPE

COLOR(S)	BRAND	DYE LOT #	SKEINS

YARN SAMPLE/LABEL

ATTACH YARN SAMPLE / LABEL HERE

SKETCH / PHOTO

	PROJECT #			HOOK
	PROJECT NAME			PATTERN
	CREATED FOR			DESIGN SOURCE
	START DATE			GAUGE
	END DATE			EXTRA TOOLS

YARN TYPE

COLOR(S)	BRAND	DYE LOT #	SKEINS

YARN SAMPLE/LABEL

ATTACH YARN SAMPLE / LABEL HERE

SKETCH / PHOTO

PROJECT #		**HOOK**	
PROJECT NAME		**PATTERN**	
CREATED FOR		**DESIGN SOURCE**	
START DATE		**GAUGE**	
END DATE		**EXTRA TOOLS**	

YARN TYPE

COLOR(S)	BRAND	DYE LOT #	SKEINS

YARN SAMPLE/LABEL

ATTACH YARN SAMPLE / LABEL HERE

SKETCH / PHOTO

PROJECT #		HOOK	
PROJECT NAME		PATTERN	
CREATED FOR		DESIGN SOURCE	
START DATE		GAUGE	
END DATE		EXTRA TOOLS	

YARN TYPE

COLOR(S)	BRAND	DYE LOT #	SKEINS

YARN SAMPLE/LABEL

ATTACH YARN SAMPLE / LABEL HERE

SKETCH / PHOTO

PROJECT #		HOOK
PROJECT NAME		PATTERN
CREATED FOR		DESIGN SOURCE
START DATE		GAUGE
END DATE		EXTRA TOOLS

YARN TYPE

COLOR(S)	BRAND	DYE LOT #	SKEINS

YARN SAMPLE/LABEL

ATTACH YARN SAMPLE / LABEL HERE

SKETCH / PHOTO

PROJECT #		HOOK	
PROJECT NAME		PATTERN	
CREATED FOR		DESIGN SOURCE	
START DATE		GAUGE	
END DATE		EXTRA TOOLS	

YARN TYPE

COLOR(S)	BRAND	DYE LOT #	SKEINS

YARN SAMPLE/LABEL

ATTACH YARN SAMPLE / LABEL HERE

SKETCH / PHOTO

PROJECT #		HOOK
PROJECT NAME		PATTERN
CREATED FOR		DESIGN SOURCE
START DATE		GAUGE
END DATE		EXTRA TOOLS

YARN TYPE

COLOR(S)	BRAND	DYE LOT #	SKEINS

YARN SAMPLE/LABEL

ATTACH YARN SAMPLE / LABEL HERE

SKETCH / PHOTO

PROJECT #		HOOK	
PROJECT NAME		PATTERN	
CREATED FOR		DESIGN SOURCE	
START DATE		GAUGE	
END DATE		EXTRA TOOLS	

YARN TYPE

✦ COLOR(S)	🏷 BRAND	▥ DYE LOT #	🧶 SKEINS

YARN SAMPLE/LABEL

ATTACH YARN SAMPLE / LABEL HERE

SKETCH / PHOTO

	PROJECT #			HOOK
	PROJECT NAME			PATTERN
	CREATED FOR			DESIGN SOURCE
	START DATE			GAUGE
	END DATE			EXTRA TOOLS

YARN TYPE

COLOR(S)	BRAND	DYE LOT #	SKEINS

YARN SAMPLE/LABEL

ATTACH YARN SAMPLE / LABEL HERE

SKETCH / PHOTO

PROJECT #		HOOK	
PROJECT NAME		PATTERN	
CREATED FOR		DESIGN SOURCE	
START DATE		GAUGE	
END DATE		EXTRA TOOLS	

YARN TYPE

✧ COLOR(S)	🏷 BRAND	||||| DYE LOT #	SKEINS

YARN SAMPLE/LABEL

ATTACH YARN SAMPLE / LABEL HERE

SKETCH / PHOTO

PROJECT #		HOOK
PROJECT NAME		PATTERN
CREATED FOR		DESIGN SOURCE
START DATE		GAUGE
END DATE		EXTRA TOOLS

YARN TYPE

COLOR(S)	BRAND	DYE LOT #	SKEINS

YARN SAMPLE/LABEL

ATTACH YARN SAMPLE / LABEL HERE

SKETCH / PHOTO

PROJECT #		HOOK	
PROJECT NAME		PATTERN	
CREATED FOR		DESIGN SOURCE	
START DATE		GAUGE	
END DATE		EXTRA TOOLS	

YARN TYPE

COLOR(S)	BRAND	DYE LOT #	SKEINS

YARN SAMPLE/LABEL

ATTACH YARN SAMPLE / LABEL HERE

SKETCH / PHOTO

	PROJECT #			HOOK
	PROJECT NAME			PATTERN
	CREATED FOR			DESIGN SOURCE
	START DATE			GAUGE
	END DATE			EXTRA TOOLS

YARN TYPE

COLOR(S)	BRAND	DYE LOT #	SKEINS

YARN SAMPLE/LABEL

ATTACH YARN SAMPLE / LABEL HERE

SKETCH / PHOTO

PROJECT #		HOOK
PROJECT NAME		PATTERN
CREATED FOR		DESIGN SOURCE
START DATE		GAUGE
END DATE		EXTRA TOOLS

YARN TYPE

COLOR(S)	BRAND	DYE LOT #	SKEINS

YARN SAMPLE/LABEL

ATTACH YARN SAMPLE / LABEL HERE

SKETCH / PHOTO

	PROJECT #			HOOK
	PROJECT NAME			PATTERN
	CREATED FOR			DESIGN SOURCE
	START DATE			GAUGE
	END DATE			EXTRA TOOLS

YARN TYPE

COLOR(S)	BRAND	DYE LOT #	SKEINS

YARN SAMPLE/LABEL

ATTACH YARN SAMPLE / LABEL HERE

SKETCH / PHOTO

PROJECT #		HOOK	
PROJECT NAME		PATTERN	
CREATED FOR		DESIGN SOURCE	
START DATE		GAUGE	
END DATE		EXTRA TOOLS	

YARN TYPE

COLOR(S)	BRAND	DYE LOT #	SKEINS

YARN SAMPLE/LABEL

ATTACH YARN SAMPLE / LABEL HERE

SKETCH / PHOTO

PROJECT #		HOOK	
PROJECT NAME		PATTERN	
CREATED FOR		DESIGN SOURCE	
START DATE		GAUGE	
END DATE		EXTRA TOOLS	

YARN TYPE

✦ COLOR(S)	🏷 BRAND	▥ DYE LOT #	🧵 SKEINS

YARN SAMPLE/LABEL

ATTACH YARN SAMPLE / LABEL HERE

SKETCH / PHOTO

	PROJECT #			HOOK
	PROJECT NAME			PATTERN
	CREATED FOR			DESIGN SOURCE
	START DATE			GAUGE
	END DATE			EXTRA TOOLS

YARN TYPE

COLOR(S)	BRAND	DYE LOT #	SKEINS

YARN SAMPLE/LABEL

ATTACH YARN SAMPLE / LABEL HERE

SKETCH / PHOTO

PROJECT #		HOOK
PROJECT NAME		PATTERN
CREATED FOR		DESIGN SOURCE
START DATE		GAUGE
END DATE		EXTRA TOOLS

YARN TYPE

COLOR(S)	BRAND	DYE LOT #	SKEINS

YARN SAMPLE/LABEL

ATTACH YARN SAMPLE / LABEL HERE

SKETCH / PHOTO

PROJECT #		HOOK
PROJECT NAME		PATTERN
CREATED FOR		DESIGN SOURCE
START DATE		GAUGE
END DATE		EXTRA TOOLS

YARN TYPE

✧ COLOR(S)	🏷 BRAND	▐█▌ DYE LOT #	🧶 SKEINS

YARN SAMPLE/LABEL

ATTACH YARN SAMPLE / LABEL HERE

SKETCH / PHOTO

	PROJECT #			HOOK
	PROJECT NAME			PATTERN
	CREATED FOR			DESIGN SOURCE
	START DATE			GAUGE
	END DATE			EXTRA TOOLS

YARN TYPE

COLOR(S)	BRAND	DYE LOT #	SKEINS

YARN SAMPLE/LABEL

ATTACH YARN SAMPLE / LABEL HERE

SKETCH / PHOTO

	PROJECT #			HOOK
	PROJECT NAME			PATTERN
	CREATED FOR			DESIGN SOURCE
	START DATE			GAUGE
	END DATE			EXTRA TOOLS

YARN TYPE

COLOR(S)	BRAND	DYE LOT #	SKEINS

YARN SAMPLE/LABEL

ATTACH YARN SAMPLE / LABEL HERE

SKETCH / PHOTO

PROJECT

PROJECT NAME

CREATED FOR

START DATE

END DATE

HOOK

PATTERN

DESIGN SOURCE

GAUGE

EXTRA TOOLS

YARN TYPE

COLOR(S)	BRAND	DYE LOT #	SKEINS

YARN SAMPLE/LABEL

ATTACH YARN SAMPLE / LABEL HERE

SKETCH / PHOTO

PROJECT #		HOOK
PROJECT NAME		PATTERN
CREATED FOR		DESIGN SOURCE
START DATE		GAUGE
END DATE		EXTRA TOOLS

YARN TYPE

COLOR(S)	BRAND	DYE LOT #	SKEINS

YARN SAMPLE/LABEL

ATTACH YARN SAMPLE / LABEL HERE

SKETCH / PHOTO

PROJECT #		HOOK	
PROJECT NAME		PATTERN	
CREATED FOR		DESIGN SOURCE	
START DATE		GAUGE	
END DATE		EXTRA TOOLS	

YARN TYPE

COLOR(S)	BRAND	DYE LOT #	SKEINS

YARN SAMPLE/LABEL

ATTACH YARN SAMPLE / LABEL HERE

SKETCH / PHOTO

PROJECT #	HOOK
PROJECT NAME	PATTERN
CREATED FOR	DESIGN SOURCE
START DATE	GAUGE
END DATE	EXTRA TOOLS

YARN TYPE

✦ COLOR(S)	🏷 BRAND	‖‖‖ DYE LOT #	🧶 SKEINS

YARN SAMPLE/LABEL

ATTACH YARN SAMPLE / LABEL HERE

SKETCH / PHOTO

PROJECT #		HOOK
PROJECT NAME		PATTERN
CREATED FOR		DESIGN SOURCE
START DATE		GAUGE
END DATE		EXTRA TOOLS

YARN TYPE

COLOR(S)	BRAND	DYE LOT #	SKEINS

YARN SAMPLE/LABEL

ATTACH YARN SAMPLE / LABEL HERE

SKETCH / PHOTO

PROJECT #		HOOK	
PROJECT NAME		PATTERN	
CREATED FOR		DESIGN SOURCE	
START DATE		GAUGE	
END DATE		EXTRA TOOLS	

YARN TYPE

COLOR(S)	BRAND	DYE LOT #	SKEINS

YARN SAMPLE/LABEL

ATTACH YARN SAMPLE / LABEL HERE

SKETCH / PHOTO

	PROJECT #			HOOK
	PROJECT NAME			PATTERN
	CREATED FOR			DESIGN SOURCE
	START DATE			GAUGE
	END DATE			EXTRA TOOLS

YARN TYPE

COLOR(S)	BRAND	DYE LOT #	SKEINS

YARN SAMPLE/LABEL

ATTACH YARN SAMPLE / LABEL HERE

SKETCH / PHOTO

PROJECT #		HOOK	
PROJECT NAME		PATTERN	
CREATED FOR		DESIGN SOURCE	
START DATE		GAUGE	
END DATE		EXTRA TOOLS	

YARN TYPE

COLOR(S)	BRAND	DYE LOT #	SKEINS

YARN SAMPLE/LABEL

ATTACH YARN SAMPLE / LABEL HERE

SKETCH / PHOTO

PROJECT #		HOOK	
PROJECT NAME		PATTERN	
CREATED FOR		DESIGN SOURCE	
START DATE		GAUGE	
END DATE		EXTRA TOOLS	

YARN TYPE

COLOR(S)	BRAND	DYE LOT #	SKEINS

YARN SAMPLE/LABEL

ATTACH YARN SAMPLE / LABEL HERE

SKETCH / PHOTO

	PROJECT #			HOOK
	PROJECT NAME			PATTERN
	CREATED FOR			DESIGN SOURCE
	START DATE			GAUGE
	END DATE			EXTRA TOOLS

YARN TYPE

COLOR(S)	BRAND	DYE LOT #	SKEINS

YARN SAMPLE/LABEL

ATTACH YARN SAMPLE / LABEL HERE

SKETCH / PHOTO

	PROJECT #			HOOK
	PROJECT NAME			PATTERN
	CREATED FOR			DESIGN SOURCE
	START DATE			GAUGE
	END DATE			EXTRA TOOLS

YARN TYPE

COLOR(S)	BRAND	DYE LOT #	SKEINS

YARN SAMPLE/LABEL

ATTACH YARN SAMPLE / LABEL HERE

SKETCH / PHOTO

	PROJECT #			HOOK
	PROJECT NAME			PATTERN
	CREATED FOR			DESIGN SOURCE
	START DATE			GAUGE
	END DATE			EXTRA TOOLS

YARN TYPE

COLOR(S)	BRAND	DYE LOT #	SKEINS

YARN SAMPLE/LABEL

ATTACH YARN SAMPLE / LABEL HERE

SKETCH / PHOTO

PROJECT #		HOOK	
PROJECT NAME		PATTERN	
CREATED FOR		DESIGN SOURCE	
START DATE		GAUGE	
END DATE		EXTRA TOOLS	

YARN TYPE

COLOR(S)	BRAND	DYE LOT #	SKEINS

YARN SAMPLE/LABEL

ATTACH YARN SAMPLE / LABEL HERE

SKETCH / PHOTO

PROJECT #		HOOK
PROJECT NAME		PATTERN
CREATED FOR		DESIGN SOURCE
START DATE		GAUGE
END DATE		EXTRA TOOLS

YARN TYPE

COLOR(S)	BRAND	DYE LOT #	SKEINS

YARN SAMPLE/LABEL

ATTACH YARN SAMPLE / LABEL HERE

SKETCH / PHOTO

	PROJECT #			HOOK
	PROJECT NAME			PATTERN
	CREATED FOR			DESIGN SOURCE
	START DATE			GAUGE
	END DATE			EXTRA TOOLS

YARN TYPE

✦ COLOR(S)	🏷 BRAND	‖‖‖ DYE LOT #	🧶 SKEINS

YARN SAMPLE/LABEL

ATTACH YARN SAMPLE / LABEL HERE

SKETCH / PHOTO

	PROJECT #			HOOK
	PROJECT NAME			PATTERN
	CREATED FOR			DESIGN SOURCE
	START DATE			GAUGE
	END DATE			EXTRA TOOLS

YARN TYPE

COLOR(S)	BRAND	DYE LOT #	SKEINS

YARN SAMPLE/LABEL

ATTACH YARN SAMPLE / LABEL HERE

SKETCH / PHOTO

	PROJECT #			HOOK
	PROJECT NAME			PATTERN
	CREATED FOR			DESIGN SOURCE
	START DATE			GAUGE
	END DATE			EXTRA TOOLS

YARN TYPE

COLOR(S)	BRAND	DYE LOT #	SKEINS

YARN SAMPLE/LABEL

ATTACH YARN SAMPLE / LABEL HERE

SKETCH / PHOTO

PROJECT #		HOOK	
PROJECT NAME		PATTERN	
CREATED FOR		DESIGN SOURCE	
START DATE		GAUGE	
END DATE		EXTRA TOOLS	

YARN TYPE

COLOR(S)	BRAND	DYE LOT #	SKEINS

YARN SAMPLE/LABEL

ATTACH YARN SAMPLE / LABEL HERE

SKETCH / PHOTO

	PROJECT #		HOOK
	PROJECT NAME		PATTERN
	CREATED FOR		DESIGN SOURCE
	START DATE		GAUGE
	END DATE		EXTRA TOOLS

YARN TYPE

COLOR(S)	BRAND	DYE LOT #	SKEINS

YARN SAMPLE/LABEL

ATTACH YARN SAMPLE / LABEL HERE

SKETCH / PHOTO

PROJECT #	HOOK
PROJECT NAME	PATTERN
CREATED FOR	DESIGN SOURCE
START DATE	GAUGE
END DATE	EXTRA TOOLS

YARN TYPE

COLOR(S)	BRAND	DYE LOT #	SKEINS

YARN SAMPLE/LABEL

ATTACH YARN SAMPLE / LABEL HERE

SKETCH / PHOTO

PROJECT

PROJECT NAME

CREATED FOR

START DATE

END DATE

HOOK

PATTERN

DESIGN SOURCE

GAUGE

EXTRA TOOLS

YARN TYPE

COLOR(S)	BRAND	DYE LOT #	SKEINS

YARN SAMPLE/LABEL

ATTACH YARN SAMPLE / LABEL HERE

SKETCH / PHOTO

Lightning Source UK Ltd.
Milton Keynes UK
UKHW031255250422
402015UK00006B/439